Rants To The Void

Deepthi H S

BookLeaf
Publishing

India | USA | UK

Made with ❤ on the BookLeaf Publishing Platform
www.bookleafpub.in
www.bookleafpub.com

Dedication

To all the puppets

Preface

This book is a collection of moments—raw, unfiltered, and deeply personal. It began as a way to make sense of the chaos within me, but it grew into something more: a mirror for anyone who has ever felt lost, broken, or unseen. These poems are my attempt to navigate the tension between light and dark, freedom and control, silence and voice. They are my rants to the void, my dances in the dark, and my whispers to the world. If you find yourself in these pages, know that you are not alone. This is for you.

Acknowledgements

This book would not exist without the support and inspiration of so many. To my family, who taught me the power of resilience and love—thank you for being my first home. To my friends, who listened to my endless rants and encouraged me to keep writing—your belief in me kept me going. To the poets and writers who came before me, whose words lit the path—thank you for showing me the way. To my readers, who find pieces of themselves in these pages—this is for you. And finally, to the void—thank you for holding space for my words, even when it felt like no one was listening.

What do I want?

Happiness?

Peace?

Satisfaction?

Purpose?

Love?

I want *everything* and *nothing* at the same time

Hot and Cold

On some days, the weather is bright and bubbly
The right temperature on the first sip of a drink
A perfect breeze - not too strong to disrupt your hair,
nor too weak to go unnoticed.

Whereas, there are other days when you stub your toe
trying to get out of bed
feeling like a wreck
Burnt toast for breakfast
and not enough will to walk out the door

Somehow having both hot and cold days
gives meaning to feeling alive

Do I owe?

A life of obedience
And resilience,
All in the name of love-
No better than a caged dove.

Freedom to choose,
But only from choices proposed.
Yet gratitude is expected,
In exchange of a life *Directed*.

I worry

I worry I won't be happy.
I worry I won't succeed.
I worry I won't understand.
I worry I won't fit in.

I worry the world will abandon me,
once my true face is perceived as ugly,
I worry that my dreams will fade to gray,
and I'll lose my way.

But here's the truth I'm starting to see:
Worry won't lend a helping hand.
It won't build my way,
nor make me stay.

So I'll take a breath, and then another,
let go of the weight, the smother.
I'll step forward, even if small,
because worry isn't my answer at all.

Hope or Control

Hope, in reality, is the worst of the evil-
The cruel light that blinds,
no better than darkness.
Feeds the idea of Control,
which is merely an illusion.

Yet still, striving for a taste of control,
to feel alive,
to feel whole.

But what if we let go?
What if we fall?
Would the absence of hope
be the greatest freedom of all?

Mirror

Is it the curiosity of wanting to explore mirror world
Or is it my desire to disappear
The mirror offers no answer,
Only the weight of question.

A world where I am whole,
or one where I am nothing at all?
The glass is cold beneath my fingertips,
a barrier or a gateway,
a promise and a threat.

I close my eyes and wonder:
If I vanish into the mirror,
will I find myself,
or lose myself forever?

Yellow Paint

When I see yellow, I am happy-
so the desperate need for making yellow
is eating me away.

I douse my brush into the sun,
paint the walls, the floors, the air,
until the world is a blur of yellow.
But the more I paint,
the more I see the cracks,
it's bleeding black.

A pair of yellow glasses
might make my world happy,
but what if it's an illusion?
What if the joy I seek
is just a filter,
a temporary fix
for a heart that aches
in every shade?

Still, I keep painting,
spreading yellow like a disease,
hoping it will infect me,
hoping it will heal me.

But the truth is this:
yellow cannot save me—
it can only remind me
of what I'm missing.

We are not that close

Dear brother,
I am not sure if watching you grow up
is a blessing or a curse.
Having you by my side is both-
a comfort and a chaos.

The endless fights,
the curses we hurl,
sometimes it feels like mom made you,
just to spite me.
But even so,
I wouldn't wish for anyone but you
as my brother.

No matter how many bridges
we burn between us,
there's always enough left
to meet each other midway.

Maybe you're not the kindest,
or the sweetest little brother,
but you are exactly the brother
I need.

Silence

Silence over company
can be the best form of therapy-
a temple for the soul,
a place to feel whole.

But silence can also be
the worst form of violence against yourself,
trapped between unspoken words,
a cage where the heart is unheard.

How can I know
when silence is healing,
and when it's concealing
the wounds that need care?

Answer?I don't know
Silence is a blank rulebook,
a double-edged sword,
a quiet storm.

So I listen closely-
to the echoes of my buried thoughts
and also ponder in the absence of sound,
Sometimes, silence is my answer,

other times, it's the question
I am too afraid to ask.

Fix you

Am I a monster?
Will I find someone who will say I am not?

See the blood on my hands—
not as stains, but as paint,
a canvas of my chaos,
a masterpiece of my mistakes.

The souls I destruct are trophies,
not of victory, but of loss,
each one a reminder
of the cost of my becoming.

Will my wounds be stitched
with threads of your hope?
Or will they fester,
raw and unhealed,
as I unravel at the seams?

Will you stay
when I can't control
this storm that devours,
just to feel the calm?

Who will be the monster in this—
me or you?
The one who destructs,
or the one who clings
to the broken pieces,
hoping to fix what cannot be fixed?

Language of Sacrifice

I was wanted in their life,
even as they were learning
to live theirs
for the first time.
Dreams were left behind
to raise me,
yet never a drop of regret
pooled in their eyes.

I would erase my existence
if it meant they could live
the lives they dreamed—
if it meant they could reclaim
the paths they left behind.

But what use would it be?
For I am the thread they chose to keep
in the tapestry of their life.
I am the colour they added,
the pattern they shaped,
a tale in their legacy.

I never believed in illusions,
but because of them,

I believe in love.
For them,
I will carry their sacrifices
as a language I speak,
a truth I live,
a debt I can never repay.

Do I resist Love?

Love exists,
As a delusion.
Has it's power only when-
It remains a mystery.
Longing for it,
Makes it believable.

For some, even finding love
among kin is a far-fetched dream.
Yet the illusion of love
is what keeps its existence alive,
a flickering flame
in the dark.

It can be argued,
To write about denial of it's presence,
One has to experience it or crave for it,
But what if love was always there,
woven into the fabric of my days,
and I turned away,
too scared to acknowledge its weight,
too afraid to feel its pull?

Did I resist love?

Yes, but not out of indifference—
out of fear.
How long can I run
from something
that has always been
a part of me?

Authentic

To be authentic
In a world of deception,
Is not easy.
To be authentic,
Is to be vulnerable.
To be the tree
That grows crooked
Because it refuses
To bend to the wind.
To be the woman,
Who lives with all
The personality traits of a man,
Even though it's socially punished
In a woman.
That's the path I choose
And I don't care
If it's not paved for me.

Thorns

19

I grew thorns,
so I am left alone.
why is it that
with more thorns,
I am wanted more?
Is it the forbiddance
that tempts?
A challenge to conquer,
rather than a cloak
to hide myself?
And if I shed my thorns,
would they still want me—
not as a challenge,
but as I am?

Distance Between Us

Life was much easier
When I ate my favourite meal made by you
Sickness vanished with your prayers
And world felt smaller and safer.
Maybe there was a reason you didn't get to see me grow
A reason I can't yet understand, but one I carry like quiet
weight.
The distance between us is just a picture frame
If I reach beyond the glass will I feel the warmth once I
knew?
The distance separates us far beyond reach
But in my memories you are closer than ever.

Unseen Strings

I feel a phantom tug,
my limbs pulled by unseen strings,
tangled and taut.
Each tug demands a performance—
a smile here,
a nod there,
a dance to rhythms I didn't choose.
I wonder:
who holds the strings?
Is it expectation,
approval,
or the fear of being cut loose?
But somewhere deep,
I feel the sharp edges,
pleading in the dark
Begging me
to snip myself free.

Cage of Comfort

I am loosing myself to the comfort
Never wanting to leave this paradise
A beautiful yet suffocating cage
The Key that sinks in my palm
While the lock masks as home
It's embrace warm
It's walls closing in
Like a hug that lasts forever
The Other side promises flying
But my mind deceives it as falling
The cage whispers
Stay here, you are safe.
But my heart beats louder
Go. You are dying here.

Barrier

We speak the same language
Yet never understand each other
We stand on the same ledge
Close enough to hold each other
Yet miles apart in meaning
The chasm between us grows
Not from lack of trying
But from the weight of what goes unsaid
Will we ever understand each other?
We may not
This barrier taunts me
With the language I can't master.

What's my worth?

A man's identity gives birth to my existence.
My honour is measured on a scale set by men,
My value decided by hands that are not my own.
I am worth only if a man decides I am worth.
Would I break this system if I were a man?
No way, cause I am no better than a man.
It all simmers down to the question I ask myself:
What's my worth?Not to him, but to me.

Drenched

I wake up to find myself in a pool of blood
Instead of horror, I feel the embrace of the thick liquid
Warm and familiar
Drenched in what should be a sin
Makes me wonder if a line exists that I have crossed
For what's it worth
I am at least smiling and not crying.

Catharsis

I am done trying
To contain the ocean within my palms
To carry the weight of every wave
That crashes inside me
Blamed by the world
For shedding my tears
Who are you to control
My own emotions spilling
Now, I am unapologetically
saying the things
I've held inside for too long.
This is my catharsis:
not a breaking,
but an unfolding.
Not a scream,
but a song.
Not an ending,
but a becoming.
And if it overwhelms you,
step back.
This is not for you.
This is for me.

Wounds

The wound that bleeds,
Deserves to heal.
Picking the scab
Or reopening the wound
To prove this cruel world
Your pain is madness.

Each time you tear it open,
you bleed anew,
and the scars grow deeper,
more jagged,
more visible.

But healing is not a performance.
It is not a spectacle
for others to witness.
It is quiet,
it is slow,
and it is yours alone.

So let it heal.
Let the skin knit itself back together,
let the ache fade into memory,
and let the scar remind you

not of the hurt,
but of the strength it took
to survive it.

Light in the void

I always felt the void
Vast and echoing my thoughts
I wondered if it's always dark
Maybe it is
But then,
why should I restrain from dancing?
In the dark
There are no one eyes to judge me,
No voice to silence my steps,
I can be me, hidden in plain sight.
Just because I thought it was dark,
Doesn't mean there was no light.
There was a light all along
I just didn't look in the right direction.

www.ingramcontent.com/pod-product-compliance
Lightning Source LLC
Chambersburg PA
CBHW071314130726

47997CB00007B/2545